NNAT®2 Practice Test – Level A (Test One)

Bright Kids NNAT®2 Practice Test – Level A (Test One)

Written and published by: Bright Kids NYC

The *Naglieri Nonverbal Ability Test – Second Edition* (NNAT®2) is a registered trademark of NCS Pearson Inc. Pearson Inc. neither endorses nor supports the content of the *Bright Kids NNAT®2 Practice Test - Level A (Test One)*.

Corporate Headquarters:
Bright Kids NYC Inc.
225 Broadway, Suite 1400
New York, NY 10007

www.brightkidsnyc.com
info@brightkidsnyc.com
917-539-4575

NNAT®2 Practice Test – Level A (Test One)

About Bright Kids NYC

Bright Kids NYC was founded in New York City to provide language arts and math enrichment for young children. Our goal is to prepare students of all ages for standardized exams through assessments, tutoring workshops, and our publications. Our philosophy is that, regardless of age, test taking is a skill that can be acquired and mastered through practice.

At Bright Kids NYC, we strive to provide the best learning materials. Our publications are truly unique. All of our books have been created by qualified psychologists, learning specialists, teachers, and staff writers. Our books have also been tested by hundreds of children in our tutoring practice. Since children can make associations that many adults cannot, testing of materials by children is a critical step towards creating successful test preparation guides. Finally, our learning specialists, teaching staff, and writers have provided practical strategies and tips to help students compete successfully on standardized exams.

Feel free to contact us if you have any questions.

Corporate Headquarters:
Bright Kids NYC Inc.
225 Broadway, Suite 1400
New York, NY 10007

www.brightkidsnyc.com
info@brightkidsnyc.com
917-539-4575

NNAT®2 Practice Test – Level A (Test One)

Introduction

Bright Kids NYC created the NNAT®2 Practice Test to familiarize students with the content and format of the NNAT®2. Students, no matter how bright they may be, do not always perform well if they are not accustomed to the format and structure of a standardized test. They can misunderstand the directions or fail to carefully read a question and properly consider all of the answer choices. Thus, without adequate preparation and familiarization, a student may not perform to the best of his or her ability on a standardized test like the NNAT®2.

The Bright Kids NNAT®2 Practice Test is not designed to generate a score or a percentile rank since the test has not been standardized with actual NNAT®2 norms and standards. The objectives of the practice test are to identify a student's strengths, weaknesses, and overall test-taking ability in order to adequately prepare him or her for the actual exam.

In order to maximize the effectiveness of the Bright Kids NNAT®2 Practice Test, it is important to first familiarize yourself with the test and its instructions. In addition, it is recommended that you work with your child in a neutral environment free of noise and clutter. Finally, a comfortable seating arrangement may help your child focus and concentrate to the best of his or her ability.

Most students will have to take numerous standardized exams throughout their school years. The best way to develop the critical thinking skills for these types of exams is to practice with similarly-styled exams under test-like conditions. This method helps ensure that a student will succeed on his or her exam.

NNAT®2 Overview

The *Naglieri Nonverbal Ability Test - Second Edition* (NNAT®2) is designed to provide a nonverbal measure of a student's general cognitive ability. Students do not use their reading, writing, or speaking skills on the NNAT®2; instead, they must rely on visual reasoning and logic to solve the problems presented to them. Since the NNAT®2 is completely nonverbal, it can be used with diverse populations of students. The NNAT®2 is an updated version of the *Naglieri Nonverbal Ability Test - Multilevel Form* (NNAT®-ML; Naglieri, 1997).

All of the information needed to solve each NNAT®2 problem is presented in the item. For example, one figural matrix format requires a student to identify what is missing in a pattern.

Figure 1: Sample NNAT®2 Question

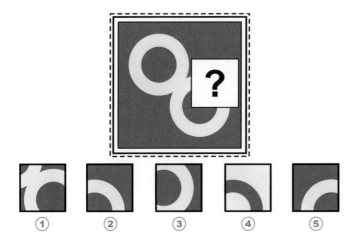

NNAT®2 scores provide an estimate of the student's cognitive ability in relation to other students of the same age. The NNAT®2 can be administered in a group or online.

The NNAT®2 is a timed test; students have 30 minutes to complete 48 questions.

NNAT®2 Practice Test – Level A (Test One)

NNAT®2 Content

The NNAT®2 is a nonverbal measure of general cognitive ability that is specifically designed to predict academic success. The student must examine the relationships among the parts of a matrix and determine the correct response based on the visual information provided within the matrix. A student must pick the correct response from five possible answer choices.

The NNAT®2 test consists of the following four question types:

1. Pattern Completion

The first question type requires a student to identify the correct piece that completes a visual pattern. These types of questions appear more on elementary level NNAT®2 tests since they are among the easiest of the matrix items.

Figure 2: Pattern Completion Example

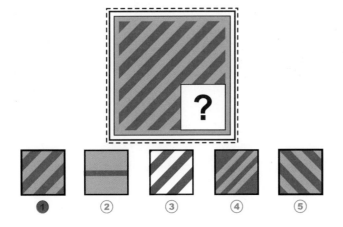

2. Reasoning by Analogy

The second question type requires a student to recognize a logical relationship between several geometric shapes to find the right answer. The student must notice how the objects in the boxes change as you move across the top row of the matrix. Then, he or she must apply the same relationship to the objects in the first box in the second row in order to determine the correct picture that belongs in place of the question mark. These items increase in difficulty when multiple changes occur across rows and columns.

Figure 3: Analogy Example

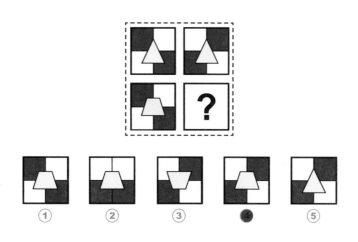

3. Serial Reasoning

The third question type requires a student to recognize a sequence of shapes and how the sequence changes across the rows and columns. For this type of question, shapes change across the rows and within the columns throughout the item. This type of matrix becomes more difficult when multiple series are included in the matrix.

Figure 4: Series Example

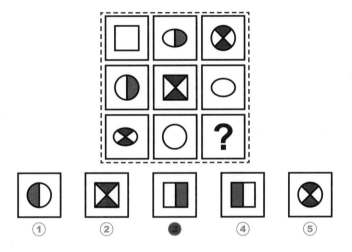

4. Spatial Visualization

The fourth question type requires a student to recognize how multiple designs would look if combined. The student must find the answer by examining the images in the boxes above and to the left of the empty box to determine what image belongs in place of the question mark. These types of questions are more complex since they involve shapes rotating or intersecting in ways that might be difficult to visualize.

Figure 5: Spatial Visualization Example

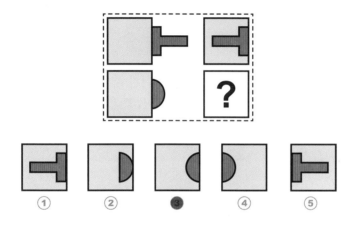

NNAT®2 Test Structure

The NNAT®2 is organized into seven levels, A through G, that are designed for students between kindergarten and twelfth grade. There are 48 questions on each level of the exam. Due to students' rapid cognitive development in earlier grades, there are separate levels for kindergarten, first, and second grade. There is one level that is for third and fourth grade and another level that is for fifth and sixth grade. The next level is appropriate for the middle school years and the transition to high school. The last level serves the last three high school grades (i.e. tenth, eleventh, and twelfth grade). See the table below for the summary of NNAT®2 test levels and their corresponding grades.

Table 1: Summary of NNAT®2 Levels and Grades

Level	Grade(s)
A	K
B	1
C	2
D	3, 4
E	5, 6
F	7, 8, 9
G	10, 11, 12

NNAT®2 Practice Test – Level A (Test One)

NNAT®2 Scoring Guidelines

The results of the NNAT®2 test comprise a wealth of useful information for test users. Derived scores based on age comparisons can be provided for all grade levels and the Naglieri Ability Index, or NAI, can be calculated for three-month intervals of chronological age. Raw scores, which are defined as the number of questions answered correctly, do not provide enough information about the quality of students' performances. However, the scaled score system connects all test levels and yields a continuous scale that can be used to compare the performances of students taking different levels of the same content cluster. Scaled scores are especially useful for evaluating changes in performance over time. Scaled scores are translated into percentile ranks and stanines in order to show the relative standings of a student in comparison to other students of the same age.

The Bright Kids NNAT®2 Practice Test can only be scored by the total number of correct answers. Since this practice test has not been standardized with NNAT®2 norms, scaled scores or percentile ranks cannot be obtained from the raw score. Please realize that a child can miss many questions on the test and still obtain a high score. Thus, it is important for this practice test to be utilized as a learning tool to help evaluate a child's strengths and weaknesses rather than to estimate a scaled score or a percentile rank.

NNAT®2 Practice Test – Level A (Test One)

How to Use this Book

This NNAT®2 Practice Test for Level A consists of 48 practice questions and an answer key.

Before you begin, it is important to familiarize yourself with the test and its instructions. You may want to take the test yourself to ensure that you can help your child review the questions he or she had difficulty solving. If your child gets frustrated, continue to provide encouragement to help him or her finish the test. Before the test, you should utilize the warm-up exercises to help your child become comfortable with matching patterns. We have also included some additional questions for students at the end of this book as a bonus challenge.

Once the test is complete, you should go over the questions and answers with your child. If the child answered a question incorrectly, he or she should verbalize what is occurring in the question or construct matrices in order to better understand the conceptual nature of the problem.

Please also review the following proven test-taking strategies to help your child succeed on the test:

1. **Listen to all of the instructions:** It is important for a student to understand the instructions for the exam and how to fill in the answer choices before he or she begins the test.

2. **Look at all of the answer choices before choosing an answer:** Since no extra credit is given for finishing the test ahead of time, it is important for a student to carefully look at all of the answer choices before selecting a final answer.

3. **Use process of elimination to get the right answer:** This is especially important if a student is unsure of how exactly to solve a problem, but can intuitively figure out the answer from the choices available to him or her.

4. **If all else fails, take a guess:** Many students skip difficult questions instead of taking an educated guess as to what the correct answer might be. Since there are no penalties for incorrect answers on this test, it is important for the student to mark down an answer before he or she moves on to the next question.

Getting Ready

Materials

1. Several No. 2 soft lead pencils, erasers, and pencil sharpeners

2. Timer or a clock

3. Ideally, a "Do Not Disturb" sign for the room where the test will be administered

Prior to Testing

1. Familiarize yourself with the practice test and the instructions. Take the practice test to make sure that you can later explain to the child why certain answers are correct or incorrect.

2. Choose a location free from distractions where you can properly administer the practice test.

3. Make sure that there is ample lighting and ventilation in the room where the practice test will be administered.

4. Complete the warm-up exercises and sample questions prior to administering the practice test.

During Testing

1. Make sure that the child knows how to accurately mark the answers.

2. Do the sample questions together to make sure the child understands the instructions. Once the sample questions are complete, do not provide any more assistance. Discuss the answers only after the testing is complete.

3. Only allow 30 minutes for the child to complete the practice test.

NNAT®2 Practice Test – Level A (Test One)

Bright Kids NYC
NNAT®2 Practice Test

Warm-up Exercises

01

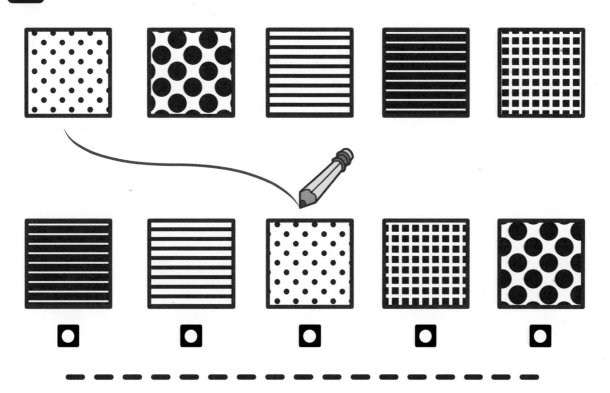

    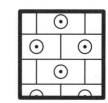

02

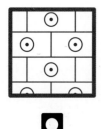 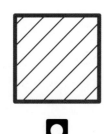   

NNAT®2 Practice Test – Level A (Test One)

03

04

05

  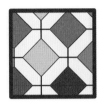 

06

NNAT®2 Practice Test – Level A (Test One)

07

    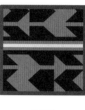

08

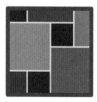    

    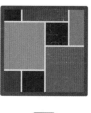

NNAT®2 Practice Test – Level A (Test One)

09

    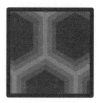

10

 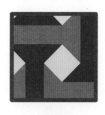   

NNAT®2 Practice Test – Level A (Test One)

Bright Kids NYC
NNAT®2 Practice Test

Level A
Test One

ISBN (978-0-9840810-9-7).

Sample Questions Administration

SAY: **Today, we are going to do some fun activities. We will do the first three activities together.**

<u>SAMPLE ONE</u>

SAY: **Look at the picture below. There is something missing. Look at the answers below and find the piece that is missing.**

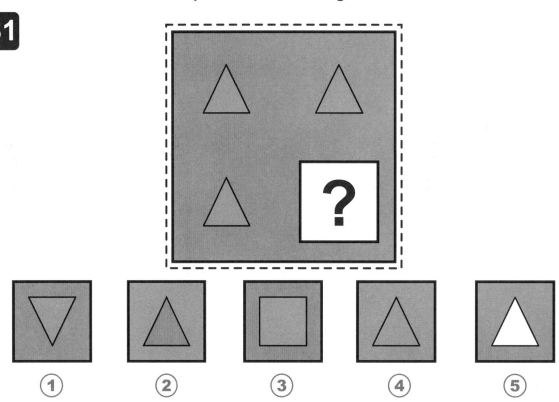

SAY: **Yes, the piece should be the green triangle inside the orange box, which is number 4. Fill in the bubble with the number "4" inside it. This is the correct answer.**

Demonstrate how to fill in the answer if the student seems confused. Remind him or her that a bubble must be visibly filled in for the question to be properly scored. Also let the student know that he or she can bubble in only one answer choice. Answer the student's questions and make sure that he or she is comfortable with the answer choice.

<u>Please note that your child may not have to bubble in the answer choices for the Level A test; he or she may just have to point to the correct answer. You will need to check with your school district to verify how the test will be administered.</u>

SAMPLE TWO

SAY: **Look at the picture below. There is something missing. Look at the answers below and find the piece that is missing.**

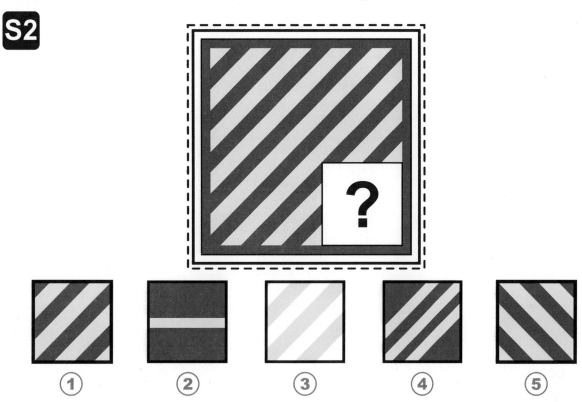

SAY: **Yes, the piece should be solid red with yellow stripes going upwards from left to right, which is number 1. Fill in the bubble with the number "1" inside it. This is the correct answer.**

Answer the child's questions and make sure that he or she is comfortable with the answer choice.

SAMPLE THREE

SAY: **Look at the picture below. There is something missing. Look at the answers below and find the piece that is missing.**

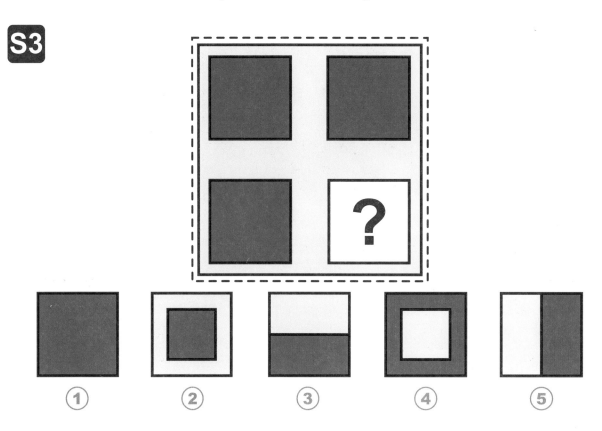

SAY: **Yes, the missing piece should be number 1. Fill in the bubble with the number "1" inside it. This is the correct answer.**

Answer the child's questions and make sure that he or she is comfortable with the answer choice.

SAY: **On the next few pages, you will be doing more activities like these. Do the best that you can with each picture and do not worry if you are not sure of all of the answers. Be sure to bubble in the whole answer space each time you mark your answer. If you want to change an answer, erase all of your first mark and mark the new answer.**

Answer the child's questions before you move on to the practice test. Once again, please note that your child may only have to point to the correct answer choice. Please check with your school district.

SAY: **Now turn the page and you may begin. I will let you know when to stop.**

Start timing and allow only 30 minutes to complete the test.

NNAT®2 Practice Test – Level A (Test One)

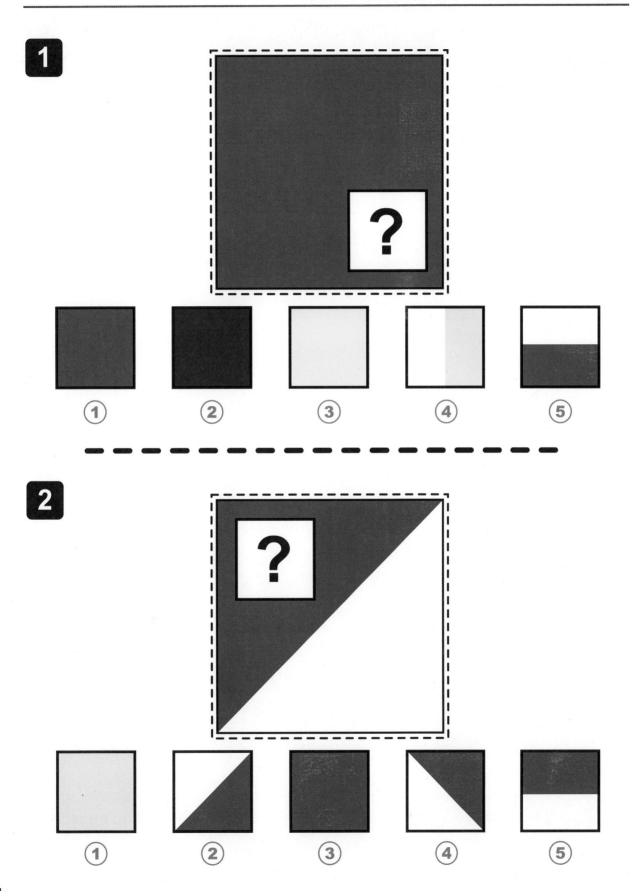

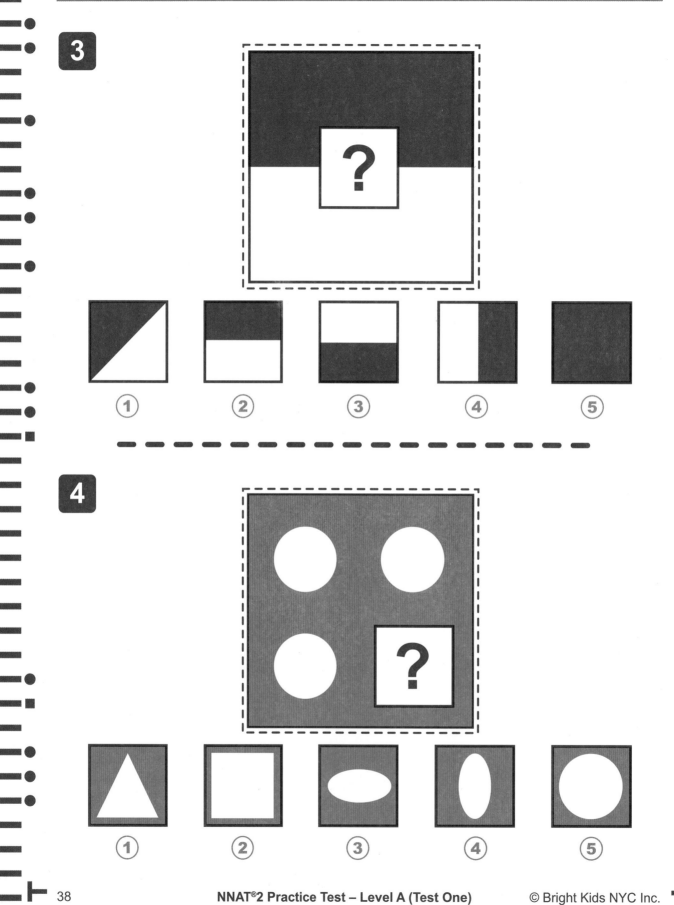

NNAT®2 Practice Test – Level A (Test One)

5

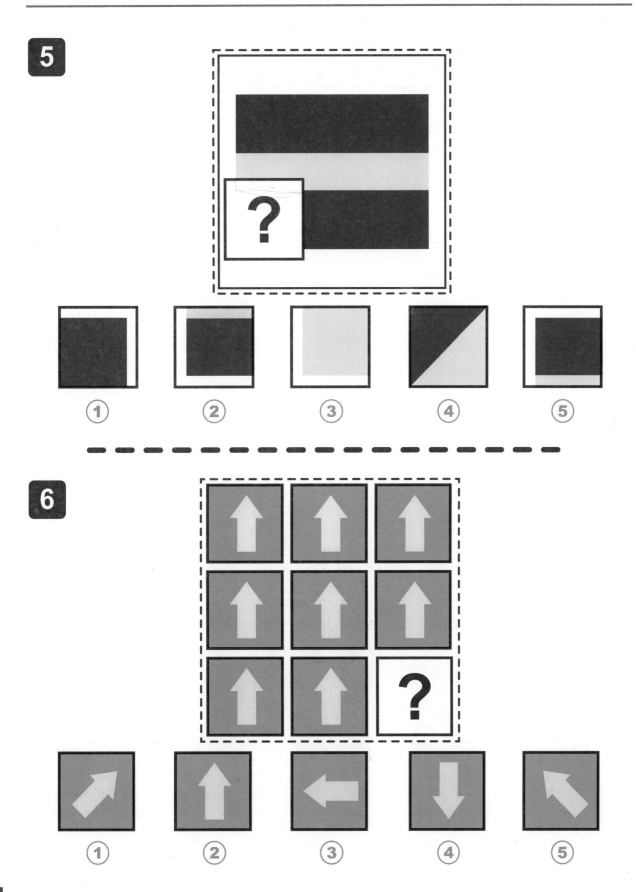

① ② ③ ④ ⑤

6

① ② ③ ④ ⑤

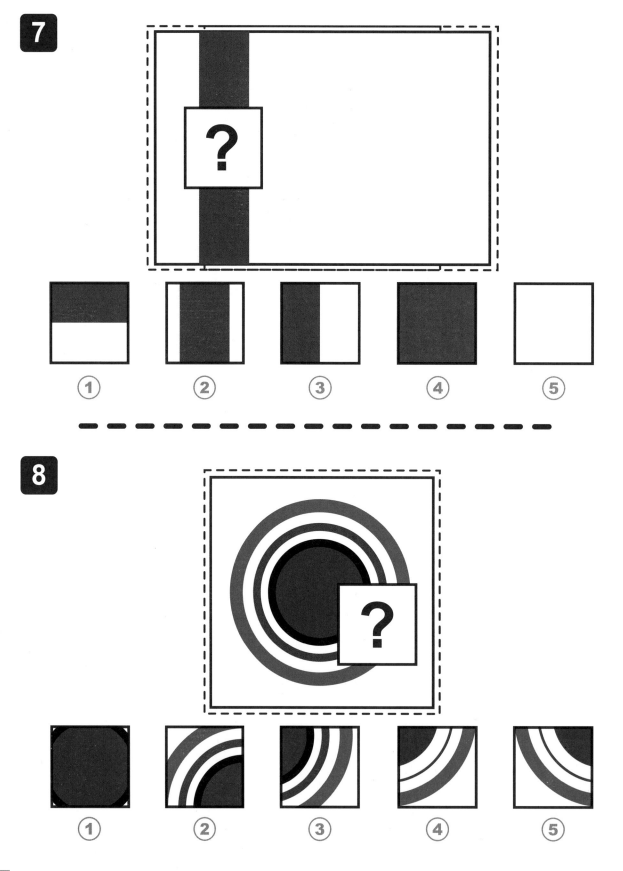

9

① ② ③ ④ ⑤

10

① ② ③ ④ ⑤

11

①   ②   ③   ④   ⑤

12

①   ②   ③   ④   ⑤

13

① ② ③ ④ ⑤

14

① ② ③ ④ ⑤

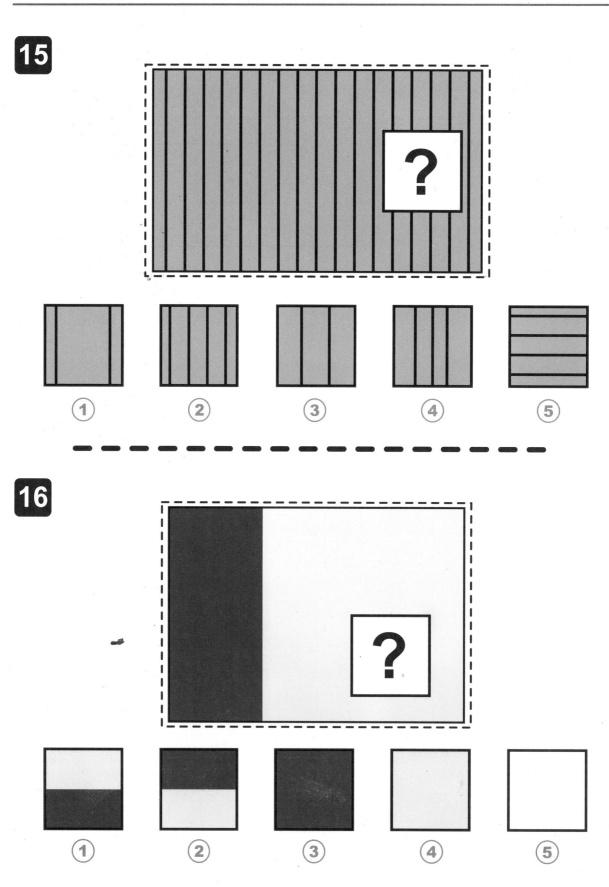

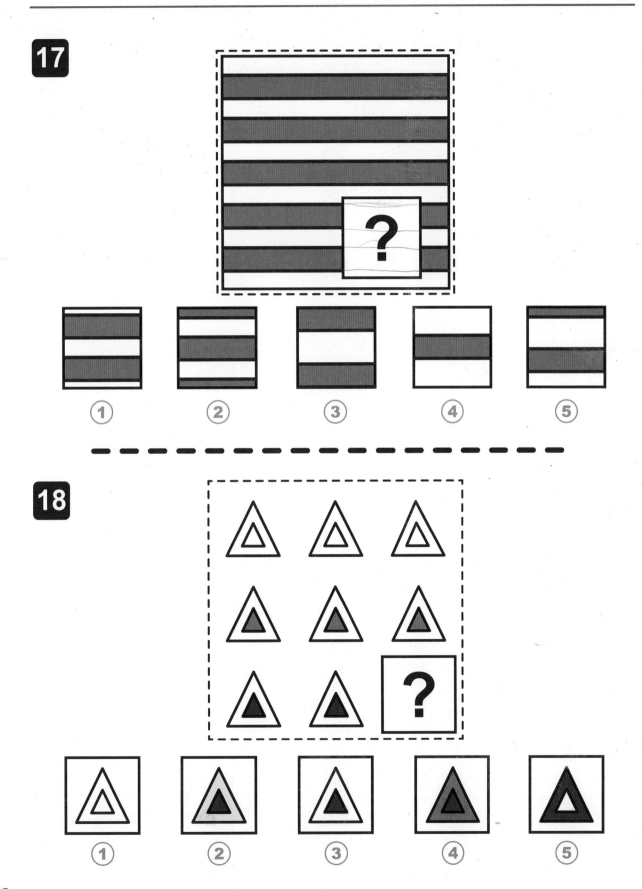

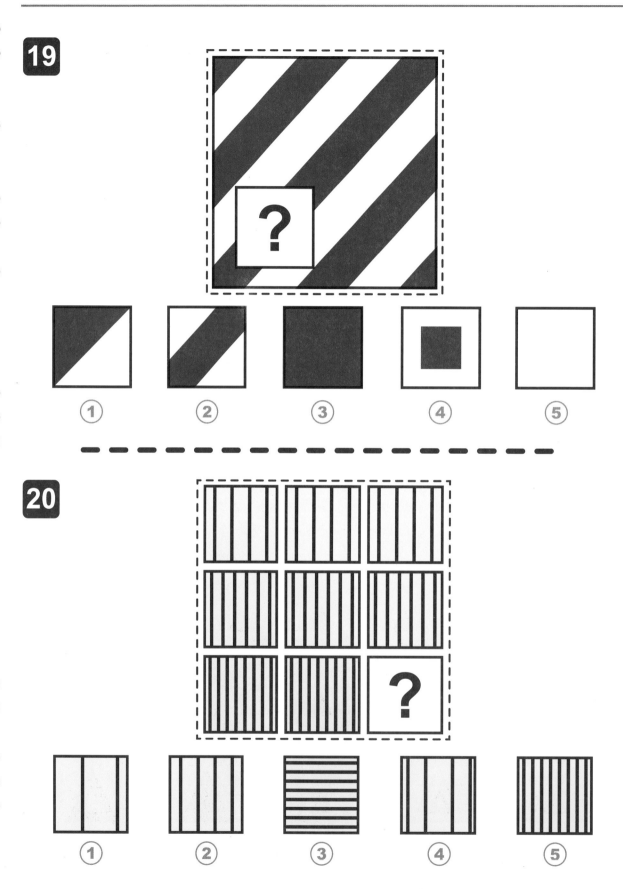

NNAT®2 Practice Test – Level A (Test One) © Bright Kids NYC Inc.

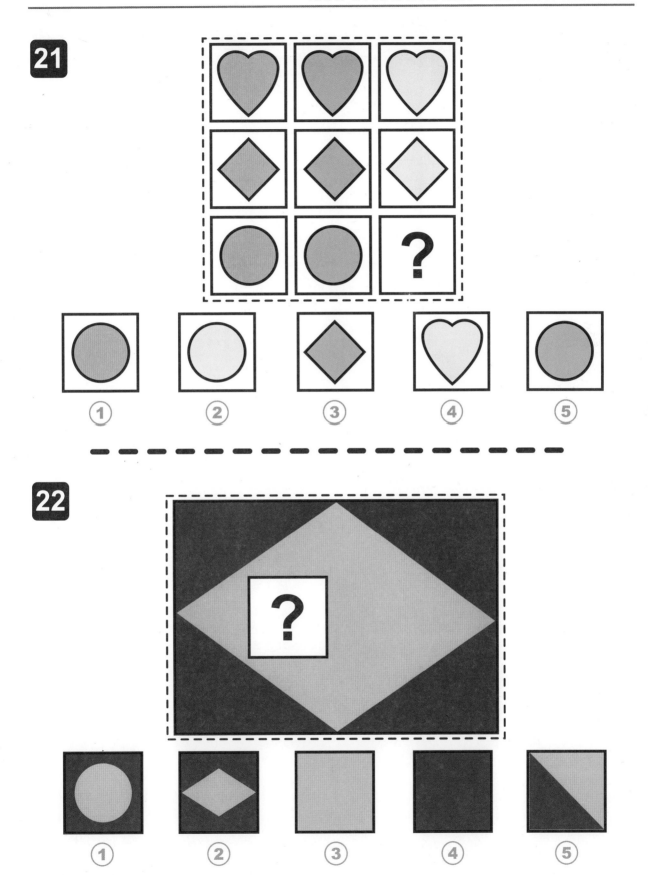

23

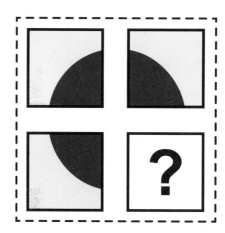

① ② ③ ④ ⑤

24

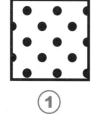

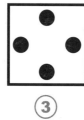
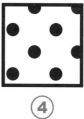

① ② ③ ④ ⑤

NNAT®2 Practice Test – Level A (Test One)

25

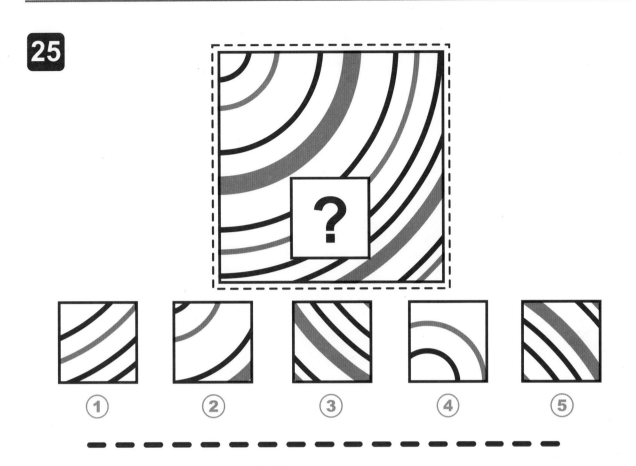

① ② ③ ④ ⑤

26

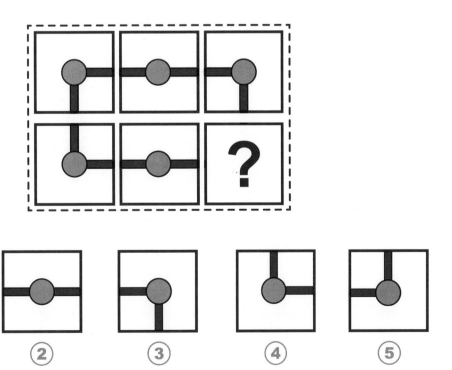

① ② ③ ④ ⑤

27

① ② ③ ④ ⑤

28

① ② ③ ④ ⑤

NNAT®2 Practice Test – Level A (Test One)

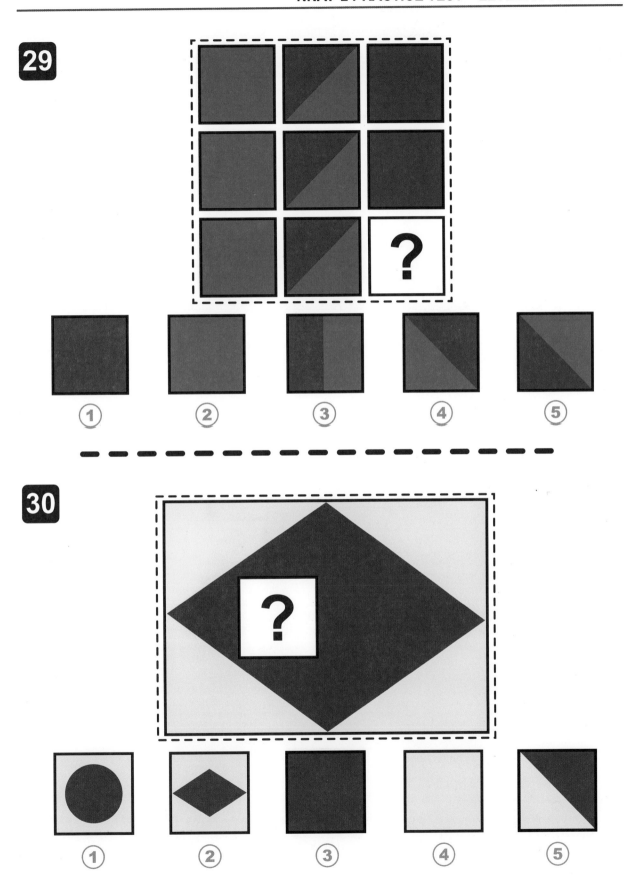

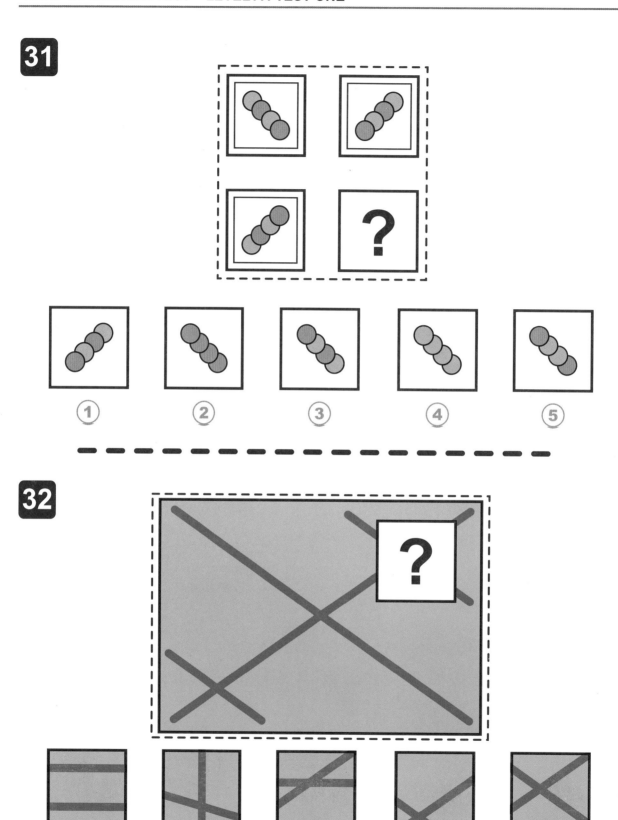

33

34

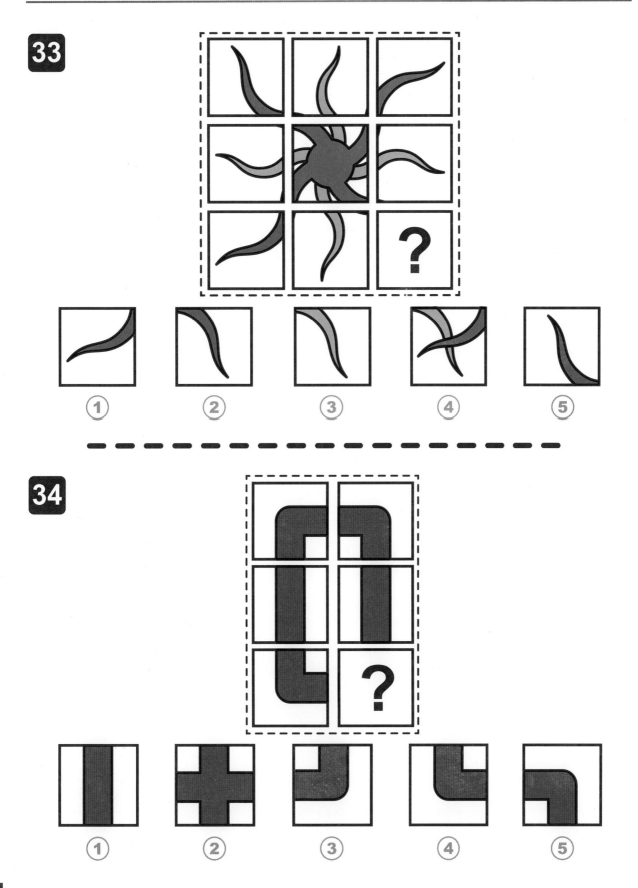

35

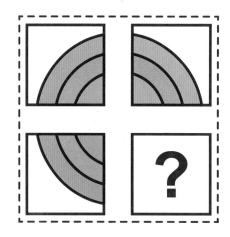

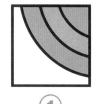

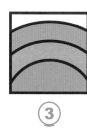

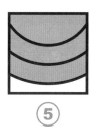

① ② ③ ④ ⑤

36

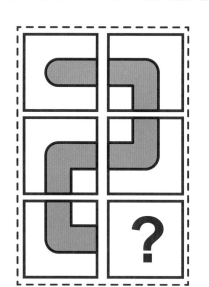

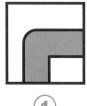

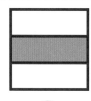

① ② ③ ④ ⑤

NNAT®2 Practice Test – Level A (Test One)

37

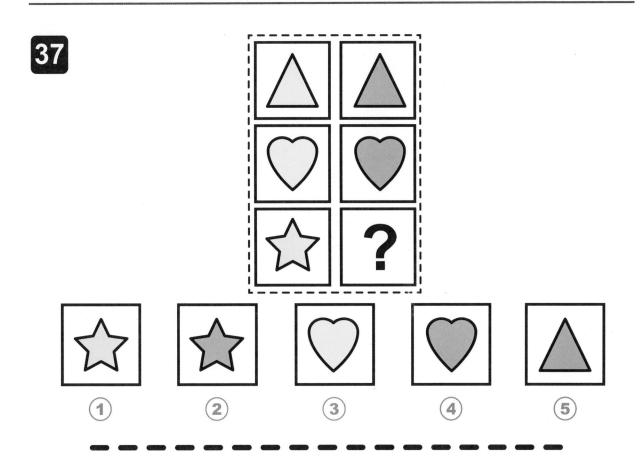

① ② ③ ④ ⑤

38

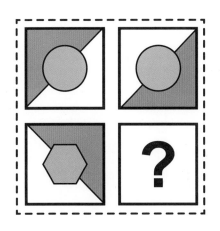

 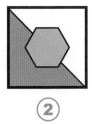 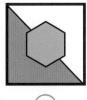 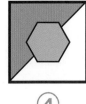 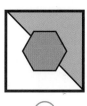

① ② ③ ④ ⑤

39

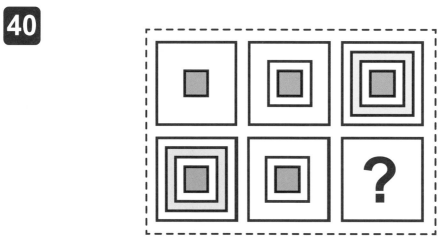

40

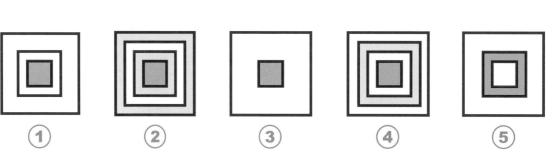

41

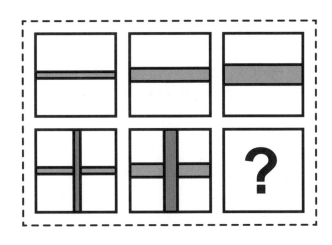

 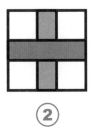 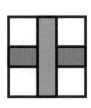 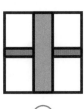

① ② ③ ④ ⑤

42

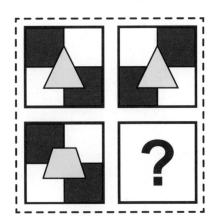

① ② ③ ④ ⑤

43

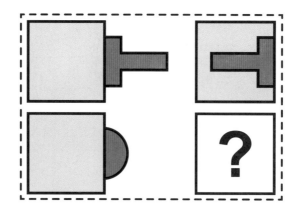

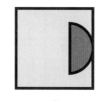
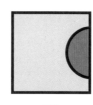
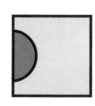
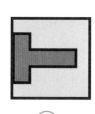

① ② ③ ④ ⑤

44

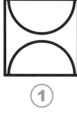

① ② ③ ④ ⑤

NNAT®2 Practice Test – Level A (Test One)

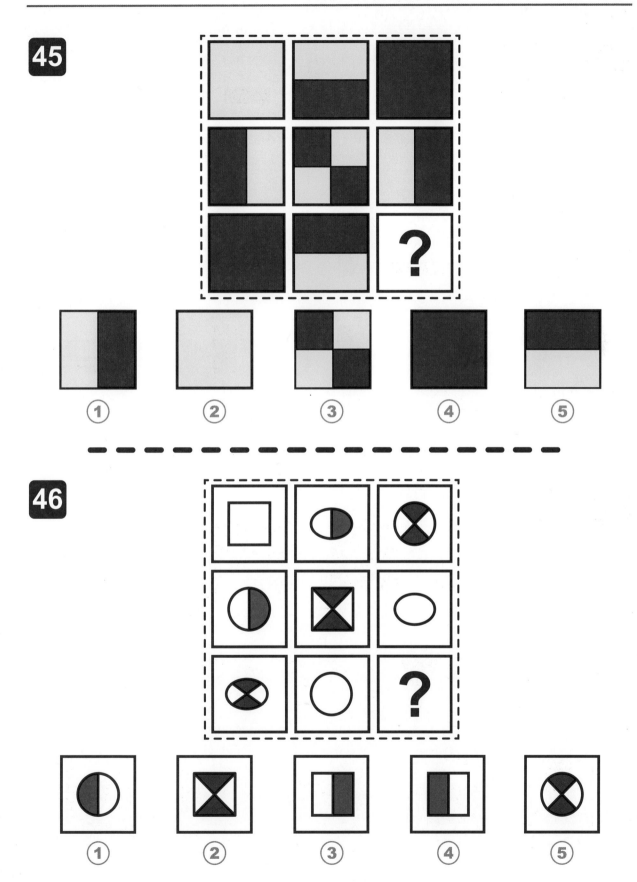

47

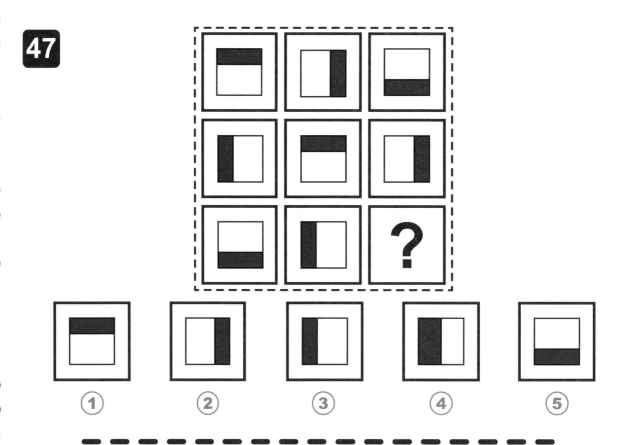

48

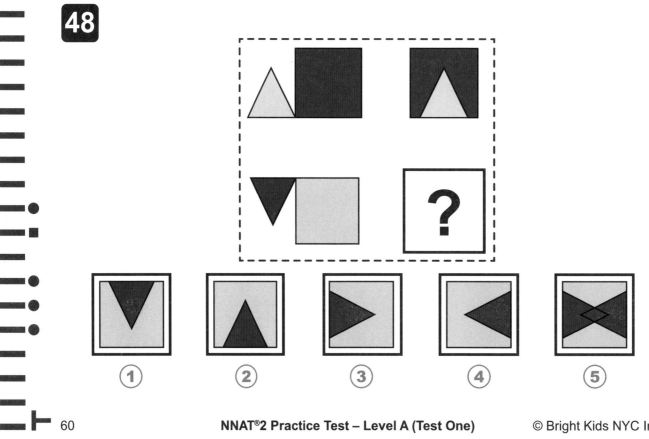

NNAT®2 Practice Test – Level A (Test One) © Bright Kids NYC Inc.

Bright Kids NYC

NNAT®2 Practice Test

Additional Questions

NNAT®2 Practice Test – Level A (Test One)

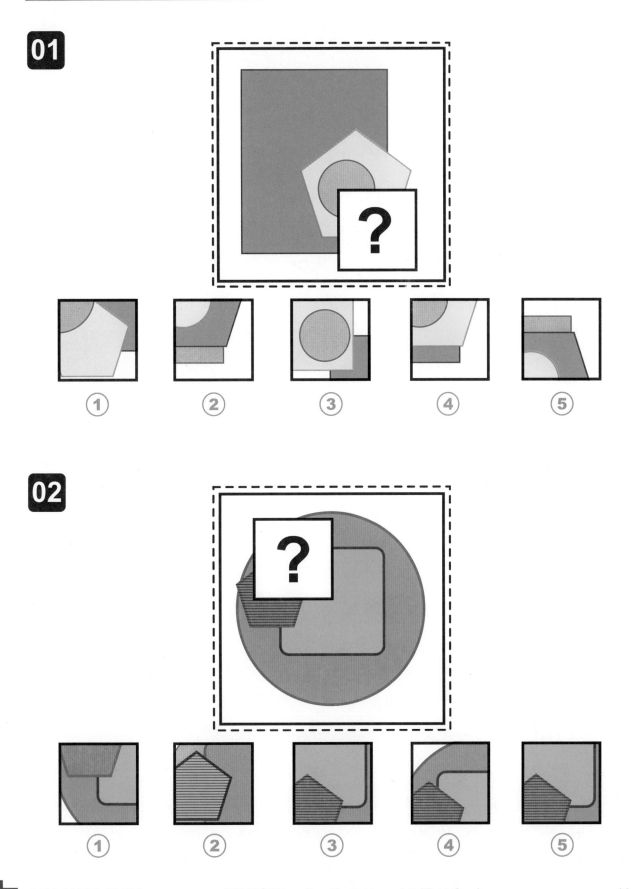

03

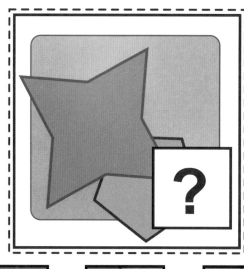

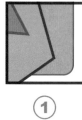   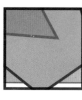   

①   ②   ③   ④   ⑤

04

   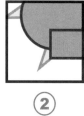   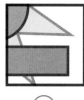   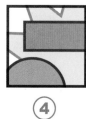   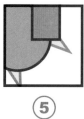

①   ②   ③   ④   ⑤

05

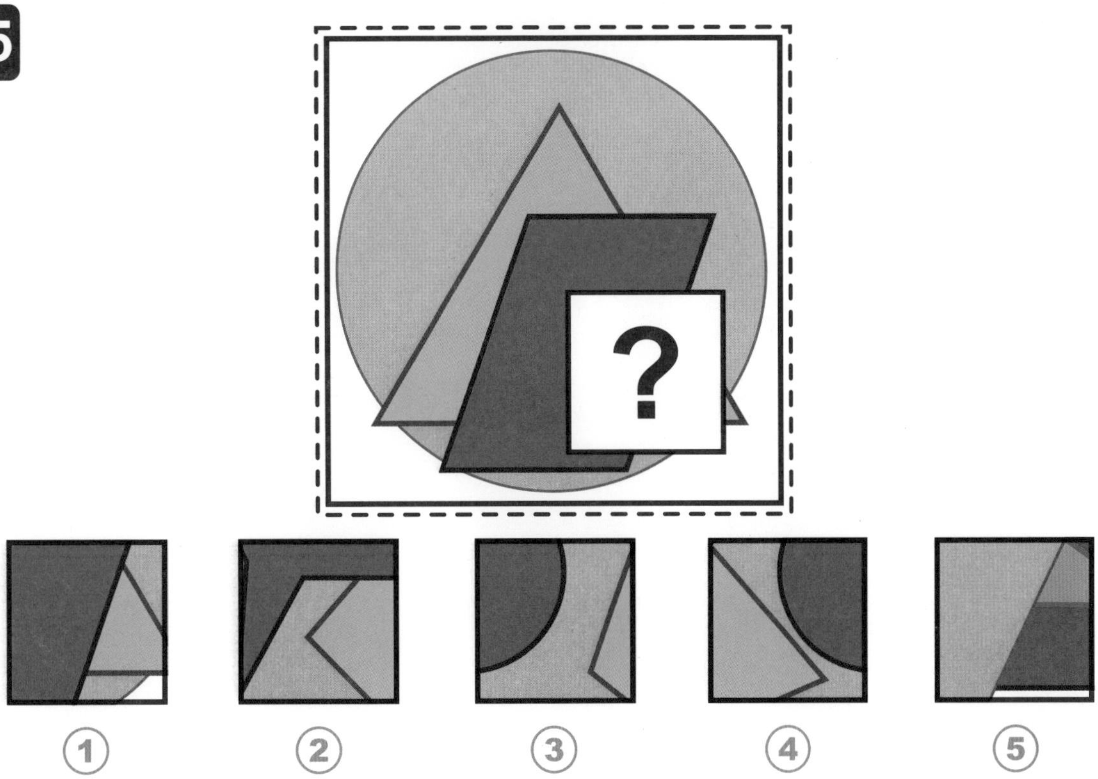

① ② ③ ④ ⑤

06

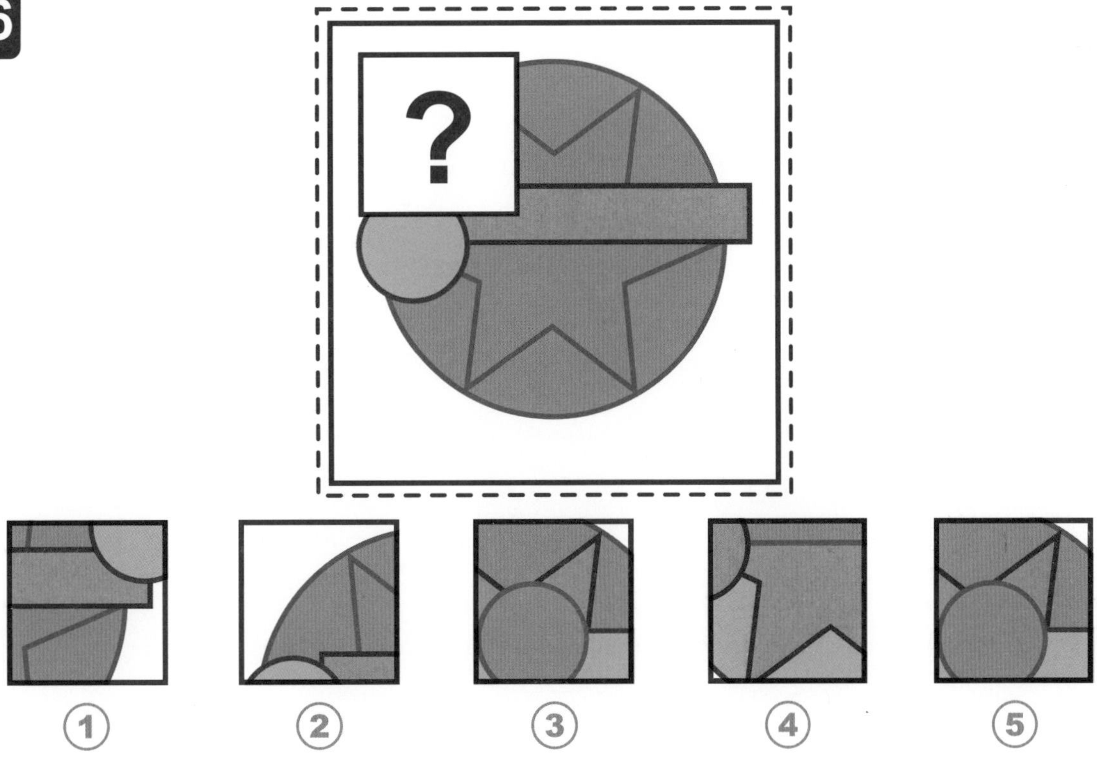

① ② ③ ④ ⑤

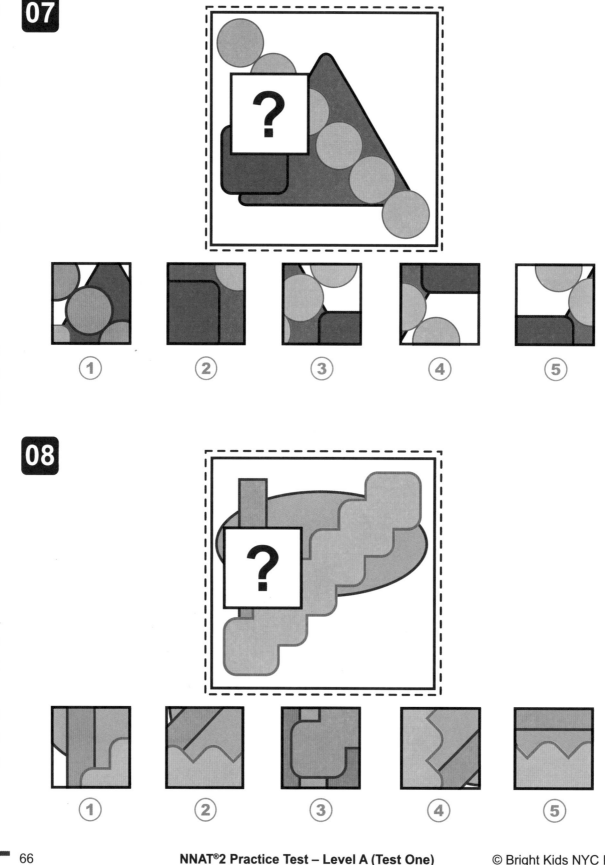

NNAT®2 Practice Test – Level A (Test One)

© Bright Kids NYC Inc.

09

① ② ③ ④ ⑤

10

① ② ③ ④ ⑤

NNAT®2 Practice Test – Level A (Test One)

NNAT®2 Practice Test – Level A (Test One)

Answer Keys

Answer Key - Level A

	Correct Answer	Student's Answer
S1	4	
S2	1	
S3	1	
1.	1	
2.	3	
3.	2	
4.	5	
5.	2	
6.	2	
7.	2	
8.	3	
9.	2	
10.	1	
11.	4	
12.	2	
13.	4	
14.	2	
15.	2	
16.	4	
17.	1	
18.	3	
19.	2	
20.	5	
21.	2	
22.	3	
23.	5	

	Correct Answer	Student's Answer
24.	1	
25.	1	
26.	5	
27.	2	
28.	4	
29.	1	
30.	3	
31.	3	
32.	5	
33.	2	
34.	3	
35.	4	
36.	4	
37.	2	
38.	2	
39.	2	
40.	3	
41.	1	
42.	4	
43.	3	
44.	1	
45.	2	
46.	3	
47.	1	
48.	1	

NNAT®2 Practice Test – Level A (Test One)

Answer Key - Additional Questions

	Correct Answer	Student's Answer
1.	4	
2.	4	
3.	1	
4.	2	
5.	1	
6.	2	
7.	5	
8.	1	
9.	2	
10.	2	

NNAT®2 Practice Test – Level A (Test One)